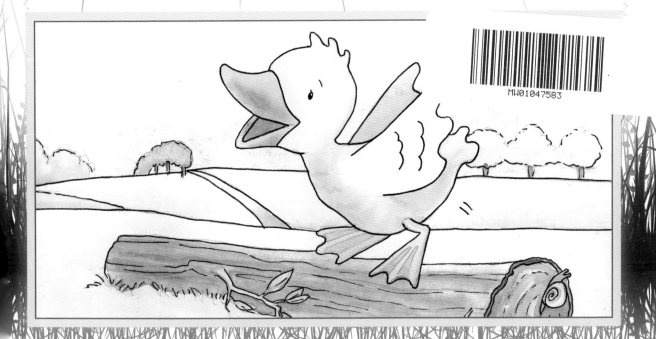

MW01047583

Quack the Duck

Written by Michèle Dufresne • Illustrated by Tracy La Rue Hohn

PIONEER VALLEY EDUCATIONAL PRESS, INC.

I am swimming.

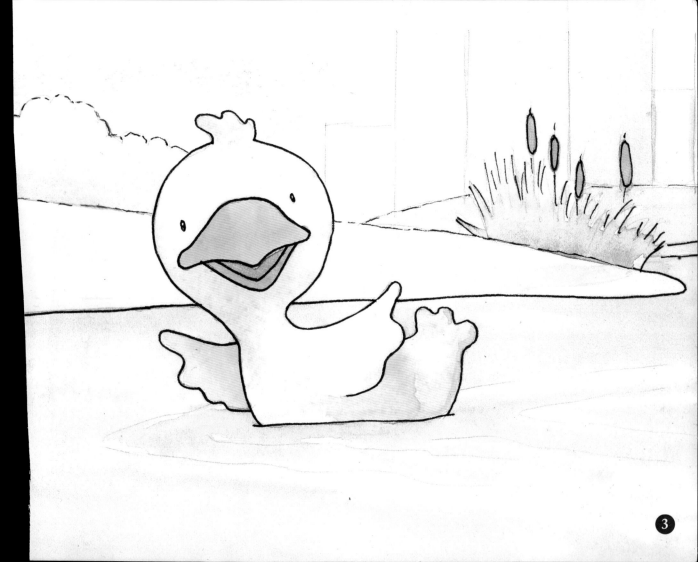

I am walking.

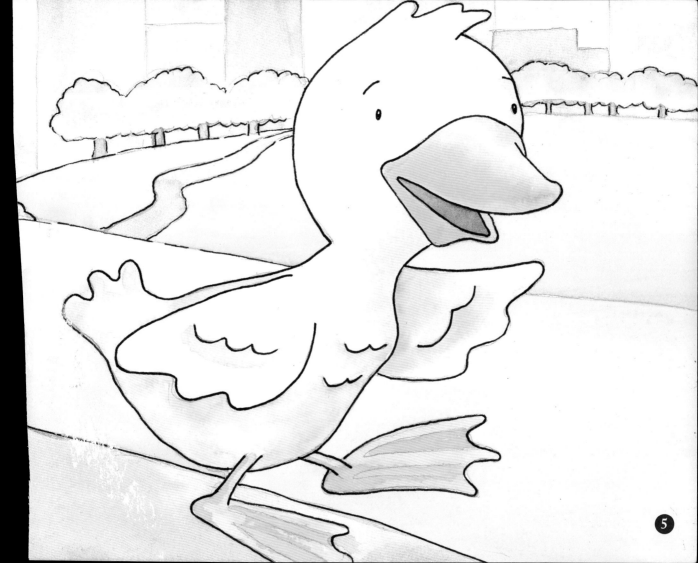

I am flying.

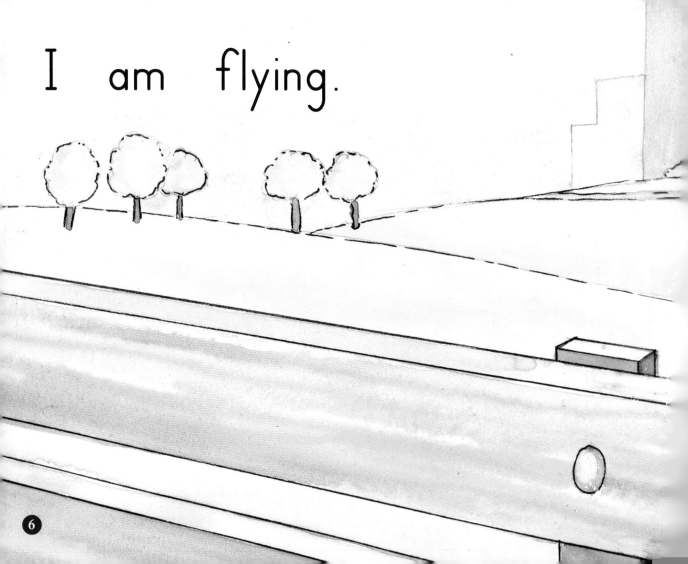

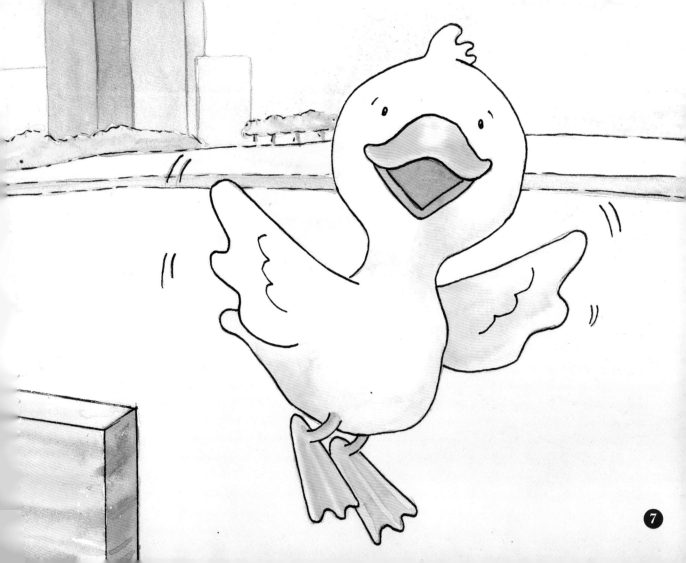

I am jumping.

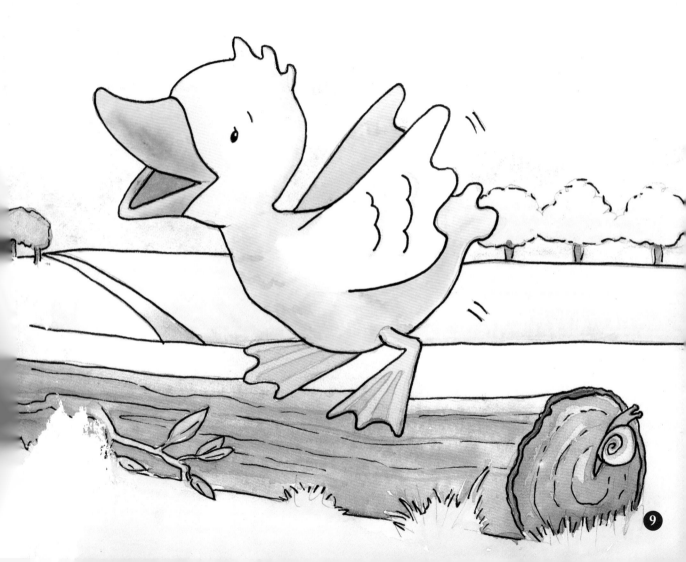

I am sleeping.

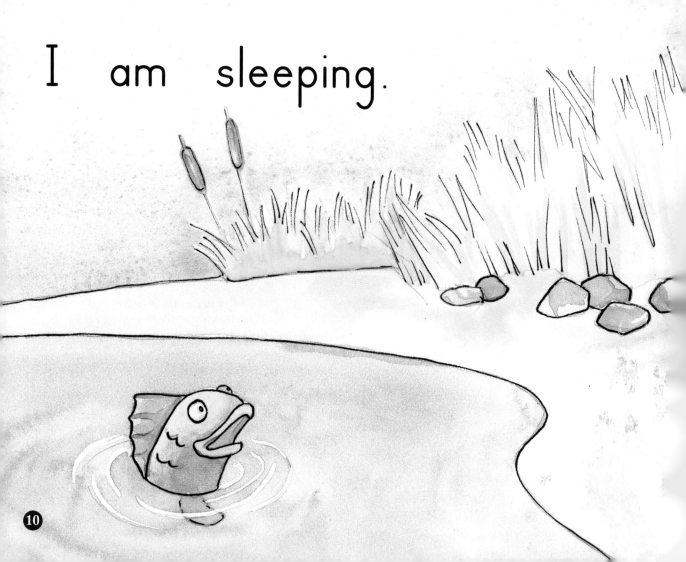

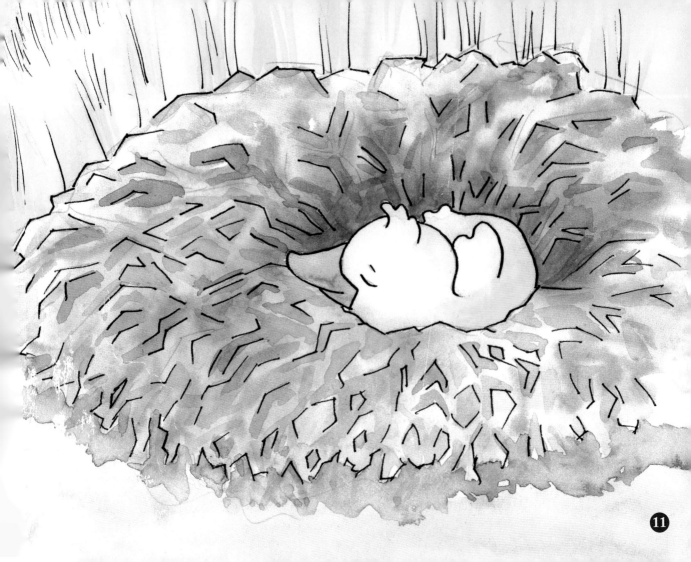

I am talking.

Quack!
Quack!